ESSAY PRESS

THE AGE OF VIRTUAL REPRODUCTION

THE AGE OF VIRTUAL REPRODUCTION / SPRING ULMER / ESSAY PRESS

Published by Essay Press 208 Utica Street Ithaca, New York 14850
www.essaypress.org Design and composition by Quemadura
Cover artwork: Eduardo Kac, *Telepresence Garment*, 1995/96.
Online telepresence work with wireless telerobotic clothes. Collection
Instituto Valenciano de Arte Moderno (IVAM), Valencia, Spain.
Printed on acid-free, recycled paper in the United States of America
ISBN 978-0-9791189-5-1 LCCN 2009925907 FIRST EDITION
5   4   3   2   1

THERE IS NO DIFFERENCE BETWEEN A HUMAN

LIFE AND A WORD. —WALTER BENJAMIN

FOR MY PARENTS

CONTENTS

I

PEASANTS (AFTER A PHOTO
BY AUGUST SANDER)

They wear suits. Someone once remarked that they do not seem
to fit them—their bodies cannot be tailored. I find their unfitted
wear beseeching. I want them in these ill-fitting suits, enjoying
their outing, looking so ephemeral. It is as if they never stopped
for a picture. History cannot remember their names, just their
bodies, just their ill-fitting suits.

I remember their faces, their unafraid eyes. They remind me
of my father in his outdated tweed dress coat and mismatching
pants, or in someone else's croquet whites, making fun of fashion, his self found in manual work, his body a blister formed from
a lifetime lifting stone.

I like the one on the left with the long nose, big eyes, slanting cane. I ignore the others. They are more posed. I will stop and talk to this one on the dirt road.

But I walk by. I think of his eyes beneath his hat and of how much younger and more attractive he is than I. I smell his smoke. It follows me like a dog. I could turn around. I do. I hold up a hand. He stops. We are within a foot or two. I have nothing to say. I gesture to my donkey. He nods. A beautiful ass, he says, taking his cigarette from his mouth.

The donkey brays.

It talks, the young farmer says.

He laughs. I blush. Is it too hot tonight to walk to the bar garden? he asks.

An innocent question. Or is it? I have lost my tongue. He pats my donkey on its forehead between its eyes. It starts, but I have hold of its rope. I am trying to convince myself of this man's arrogance, trying to make of him an enemy, find fault with one of his features.

Well, I better catch up with them, he says, cocking his head in the direction of his friends.

Ciao, I say, and raise my hand again.

For many days, whenever I pass this dip in the road, I look for him. I dress in my favorite clothes.

*Their hands look too big, their bodies too thin, their legs too short.
(They use their walking sticks as though they were driving cattle.)*

WIM WENDERS AND THE SUIT THAT FIT HIM

In *Notebooks on Cities and Clothes*, Wenders films clothing designer Yohji Yamamoto at work on his new fall line. Yamamoto cuts entire outfits loose with scissors, tearing at them ununiformly. Wenders does the same, cutting his film at odd intersections to suggest that both artists' creative processes are the same. *I was too quick to put fashion down*, Wenders narrates. *Why not look at it ... like any other industry, like the movies for example? Filmmaking ... should just remain a way of life sometimes, like taking a walk, reading a newspaper, eating, writing notes, driving a car or shooting this film here.*

The film begins after Wenders buys a suit carrying Yamamoto's label. *I felt protected like a knight in his armor—by what, a shirt and a jacket?* Wenders asks. *This jacket reminded me of my childhood and my father as if the essence of this memory were tailored into it ... What did Yamamoto know about me—about everybody?*

Yamamoto: *Well, sometimes I don't care if no one understands me.*

WHAT SANDER SAW

Three young men
on their way to a dance,
on their way from country to city,
on their way from childhood to battlefield,
reeking of melancholy.

MY FATHER'S BLACK HOODIE

From an early age, I fashioned myself after my father (I wore a
black sweatshirt for most of my adolescence), after his Carhartts,
his fashion faux pas. Today I wear a blue hoodie. It is thermal,
cuffs raveled. Its holes aren't real holes—they don't go all the way
through the lining. My undershirt is flowered, coffee-stained,
pants a washed-out grey. This is my uniform. I don't clean up. I
grew up in the woods where clothes need to get dirty and with-
stand wear. My pant cuffs are too long, though. They drag and I
walk on them. I like walking on them.

I am interested in how clothes fit us or don't. I like to be able,
for instance, to hide in my clothes. Other times, I like them to
show me off. The peasants in their suits remind me of eighth
grade, my first expensive dress, black with a drop waist. I wore a
white silky blouse beneath. My sudden need to appear sophisti-
cated.

Berger on Sander again: *His full aim was to find, around Cologne in the area in which he was born in 1876, archetypes to represent every possible type, social class, sub-class, job, vocation, privilege. He hoped to take, in all, 600 portraits. His project was cut short by Hitler's Third Reich.*

An artist's lifework cut short by Hitler's genocidal agenda of cataloguing types—a cataloguing that can be traced back to the early European interest in relationships between the facial angles of monkeys and humans. The less intensely inclined the facial angle, it was argued, the smaller the brain. This misconception encouraged certain idealizations of the severely inclined Aryan facial angle and, in turn, the criminalization of all other craniofacial features.

Some scholars contrast Hitler's adherence to 'fixed physiognomy' (reading the shape of the skull) with Sander's adherence to the notion of 'mobile physiognomy' (reading the shape of one's physique) as a way to define character. But how then to explain Sander's photograph of a man in profile titled *The Criminal Type*, not to mention Sander's talk of his project as a physiognomic one akin to 'facial reading,' which, he argued, was *an ancient language*?

The question of how influenced Sander was by racist physiognomic theories aside, he was inspired by various new thinkers of
his times, like Oswald Spengler and the Cologne Progressives.
Sander subscribed to Spengler's theory that all great cultures are
rooted in the countryside, evolve from barter societies to urban
markets, and eventually collapse into soulless bureaucracies. He
was likewise intrigued by the Cologne Progressives' painterly
practice of reducing the human figure to an abstract type in an
effort to comment artistically upon the alienating effects of capitalism. In time, Sander's project, *Men of the 20th Century*, developed into a series of portraits divided into groups that he believed
represented *a truthful outline of the existing social order*. In the early
1930s, he added both the Nazi and Jew to the groups in this catalogue. Soon, his work was lambasted by the Right as being *a physiognomic document of anarchy, of inferior instincts and of indiscrimi-
nate greed, rather than a document of uplift, enthusiasm, let alone
essence*, and in 1936, Nazi authorities destroyed his halftones.

Secreting his negatives away in the countryside, Sander
worked there for years ordering his oeuvre, ending it finally with
a photograph of his son Erich's death mask. I keep returning to
this photo, taken after Erich died in a concentration camp, as this
shot, not to mention a preceding image titled *Political Prisoner* of
Erich sitting at a desk in his camp uniform, so clearly tell the story
of the prescient failure of Sander's project. Both the photo of his
son as a political prisoner and the shot of his son's death mask

ruin the archetypal reading of the other hundreds of people he photographed, reminding us that each one of his sitters are individuals' sons and daughters. Not exactly Sander's intention for his catalogue. Or was it?

Sander put people in the city *and* the country at ease. He learned this skill, I surmise, transitioning from peasant (he was born and reared in a rural German mining community) to citified man. The limit of Sander's social vision, however, is best examined by reading his description of those he calls circus people: *This is a class of people which, with a few exceptions, now belongs to the past ... It is very interesting to talk to these people: one learns a great deal about their circumstances and the deeper meaning of their lives. I wish to give neither a critique nor a description of these people, but only to create a piece of contemporary history with my pictures, a little romance in a materialistic age.*

Was Sander's real love, then, romancing the past? The singular beauty of his images of peasants and the working class, and his attention to rendering these people in the best possible light, does indeed outshine the attention he paid everyone else. I wonder whether he ever fully recognized his own romantic obsession with what was disappearing. I imagine he did, and that his entire megalomaniacal project was an attempt to capture this vanishing life before it was too late.

Peasants are on the edge of extinction—an extinction Sander feared was occurring in the early twentieth-century, but which John Berger argues takes place later with the advent of monopoly capital, multinational corporations, agribusiness, and globalization.

I grew up in a family that embraced peasant life. It was not a simple embrace. My parents poured sweat into building their own home, share-cropped tobacco, and grew a large garden they peddled at urban markets. When I turned nine, they rented out our house, withdrew their entire savings from the bank, and took me to a place where peasantry still existed. For five months that year I bicycled more than 3,000 kilometers around Greece with them, sleeping in barns, spare bedrooms, on pieces of styrofoam that reeked of cat-piss, in a tent, and in the occasional pension complete with feather beds and hot chocolate in the morning.

Berger explains that he, like my parents, chose to live the peasant life, and that the choice was a privilege, as he was exempt *from those necessities* which determine most peasants' lives. But he is quick to remark that the peasant life within corporate capitalism is one of exploitation and oppression. It's a life that should not be romanticized, maintained, or preserved in its current form. He argues, though, that the peasant mindset (in particular, the wariness with which peasants perceive globalization) is something to be emulated.

April asked.

I said, It comes from growing up a certain way. It comes from my parents building their first house for less than $1,000 when they were my age. Then I spoke of feeling animosity toward those who ask if my parents were hippies, and of the way some people try to sweep my lifestyle, the one with which I was reared, under the carpet, saying, Why don't you go back to your cave? These persons have preconceptions about living off the grid. I do too, but I also know how I lived off the grid. And this is what I yearn to return to.

I want to build a house, I said. I have to. Besides, it would make my father happy. That's reason enough. It's like building a boat. If you have to build a boat, then you have to build a boat. Some people just have to. Then they do. I might build a house, live in it for two years, and then say, 'Okay.' I would have done it. Tried to live that way. I would no longer be afraid of doing it.

Part of the rub, though, is that I can't just replicate my childhood. I have to make the venture mine, not my parents'. I have to find me in the act. My folks would love it if I inherited their love for the land, if I gardened and got up wood. Then, too, there is my father's stonework—a dying craft that will die a little more when he passes. (Two summers ago, I built a school in Rwanda out of block, and I dreamed, then, of building my own home. It was the sweetest dream. I also dreamed of a slab of black granite.)

=

Maybe you have to go home and build a house near your parents, Nancy (who was also listening) said.

I shivered because she said it point blank. And I shivered because I had just written a letter to my parents saying that I was applying for jobs near them and then almost hadn't mailed it, because making such a statement is like moving there already—they want me to move there so badly and I've always resisted. But I feel something changing inside myself, I later told April, driving downtown, describing to her the condition of my father's illness. My mother, too, collapsing.

A BODY SPEAKS

The accident of Sander's image of the three farmers on their way to a dance is that the three men's heads all rest perfectly along the horizon. This rare symmetry is then magnified by their dress shoes, all angled perfectly upon the oddly glistening path. I wait for the one whose cane and cigarette glow white. Of the three, he looks the kindest, though I know better than to judge by looks alone. Still, why does his face *speak* to me?

I read his face, yet he can't read mine. Rather, he reads Sander's. (Sander came to this dip in the road, this juncture, in 1914, and was changed by the encounter. Changed because these young farmers stared back at him, and the virility of their gaze filled with adolescent verve altered the way he thereafter engaged his subjects, opening his eyes to a more reciprocal way of seeing.)

In my daydream, this young farmer with the long nose makes it back from the Great War, stumbling over the 40 million dead, and appears here where I've waited for years. He acknowledges me with a small wave.

My donkey brays.

WIM WENDERS AND YOHJI YAMAMOTO TAKE TWO

Wenders: *Yohji's Tokyo office was brimming with photos and images stuck to the walls . . . And his shelves were cluttered with photo books, among which I discovered one which I know and treasured as much as he: 'Men of the 20th Century' by August Sander . . .*

Yamamoto: *I'm especially curious about their faces, because of their career, life, business. They have exactly the right faces for that [pointing to Sander's rotund 'Pastry Chef'] . . . I'm admiring their faces and clothing . . . Their clothes, too, are clearly representing their business, their life . . .*

People today don't look like their profession, Yamamoto adds, refusing Sander credit for having searched out the perfect subject to fit each professional archetype. Rather, Yamamoto chooses to believe the myth Sander presents: that the dress makes the man or at least defines him.

In Yamamoto's Spring 2008 ready-to-wear line, I spy a woman's blazer with front pockets cut just beneath the model's ribs. The model stands, hands in pockets, looking not unlike one of Sander's subjects whose hands are often slipped in between the front buttons of their double-breasted suits.

POCKETING THE SCENE

You are my pocket, I tell the farmer, returned from war, face weathered.

And you're my ass, he says, a smile crinkling the crows of his eyes.

I laugh. The sun is setting. I look up at the purple sky. My farmer lifts his arms and shakes off his coat. It's the same coat he was wearing when I first laid eyes on him. The ripped armpits endear me. He covers us both with it as we recline onto the cold, slightly damp ground. Through its holes, I can see the Pleiades. When I turn my head, all I can see of my farmer are his eyewhites. Then he closes his eyes.

ZACH

I sit here thinking about you, and what it means to lose the love of your life. I am not sure we ever recover. Your vulnerability makes me try all the harder to articulate why it is, for me, that you've come to signify the epitome of such loss. You were born with blood in your brain. Kicking and screaming, you shrank from touch. At two, you were diagnosed with autism, and at eleven, you fell in love with a potbellied pig named Sid. I don't know the details of your and Sid's relation, I only know what a pig's skin feels like: sandpaper if rubbed the wrong way. And how a pig sounds while rooting: like a birthday noisemaker that unfurls into a long paper tongue.

I understand that routine for you, an autistic child, is important and that the slightest irregularity is upsetting, so I can only imagine your grief the day Dakota City, Iowa, ruled that your pig, Sid, violated the city's livestock ordinance and banished him to a barn on the outskirts of town. For weeks after this, your mother said, you didn't understand Sid was gone and went expectantly to the window where you used to play hide and seek with him.

Far away in a barn, Sid grew sick and lost weight. A professor came, took a look, said pigs are fairly sociable animals and that the problem was that Sid was basically in solitary confinement out there, and that this wasn't good for any pig's mental health.

Temple Grandin, who is autistic like you, writes, among other things, about how domestic animals need companionship. When they are young, especially, they need not only the heat of their mothers' bodies, but social contact to stay emotionally warm. Without social interaction, animals develop abnormal behaviors like rocking and pacing, grow overly excitable, and engage in acts of self-mutilation.

Prisoners in solitary react similarly. Arthur Koestler, for instance, while in a Spanish cell awaiting death, paced back and forth. Everything became for him a measurement and each movement symbolic. To cross his cell and back took six and a half paces. He took care not to step on any crack but placed his feet carefully in the middle of the flagstones. After pacing back and forth five times, he always felt assured he would be released. And, as it happened, he was.

I understand this. I wasn't in solitary, but at eighteen I became anorexic, sequestering myself and rationing everything from my caloric intake down to what exact fork I had to use if I was to eat anything. It was during this particularly challenging and auspicious time that I also experienced something of the loss of the self that Koestler experienced. The best way to explain this phenomenon to you, Zach, is to tell you that as I grew thinner, I began drawing pictures of myself whispering to myself. Koestler calls such split-consciousness a dream-like state of *dazed self-estrangement,* and testifies that while in solitary confinement, at certain moments his 'I' ceased to exist and he felt like he was *in touch with 'real reality.'* Afterward, he writes, *there remained a sustained and invigorating, serene and fear-dispelling after-effect that lasted for hours.*

Temple Grandin testifies to being flooded with a similar state of calm after being held in a squeeze chair she invented. The chair—modeled after cattle chutes which calm animals down by applying pressure to their bodies as they are shuttled to slaughter—looks like a piece of playground equipment. You lie in it on your stomach, Zach, and the padded plywood panels press in on you.

Grandin's squeeze chair hugs her without violating her autistic need to shrink from human touch. When she's in the squeeze chair, she says, her anxiety disappears and she is able to feel comfortable in her own skin. New studies show both anorexia and autism are neurological conditions that can be attributed to genetic make-up. Like people with autism, anorexics have high opioid (endorphin) levels in their brains and suffer from touch deprivation as children and adults. An opioid blocker—the drug naltrexone—thought to increase the need for social desire, has been given to both anorexics and persons with autism, but the results, especially for anorexics, are somewhat mixed. Therapies, however, in which anorexics are held and rocked have proven highly effective, if difficult to practice. Montreux, a clinic in Canada in which patients were hugged and rocked by caregivers in rocking chairs, had a phenomenal recovery rate, but lost its license after health officials claimed it violated patients' rights. From the nice feelings the chair gives her, she has learned to give such feelings to animals by holding them. In other words, the squeeze chair has taught her a kind of empathy. Without the chair, she writes, she would be *a cold hard rock*. But even given the chair, Grandin leads a celibate life. (She has never fallen in love and does not understand complex human emotions.) Now the premier designer of 'humane slaughter facilities,' she believes animals should die painlessly and claims the closest she's come to feeling love is while holding an animal at the moment of its painless, chuted death.

This experience of Grandin's reminds me of a passage by Jean Genet in which he writes about female animals and their dead offspring, arguing that the passion with which these animals hold onto their dead is what love is: *consciousness of the division of what previously was one, of what it is to be thus divided, while you yourself are watching yourself.*

All this may seem confusing to you, Zach. But what it makes me think is that people like you and those in solitary (and maybe me and others who deny themselves) need more than physical contact—be it the touch of a chair, animal, or human—to keep warm. We need love. Maybe because you are now missing Sid so terribly, you can understand what I mean.

My learning to love is linked in my memory with my last visit to the Vermont woods where I was reared. On this visit, I was not alone. I was holding a man's hand. I remember being bowled over by a feeling of completeness as the trees bowed to us. It was winter. I felt slightly dizzy. My lover and I stood for some time in silence. Then we walked around the house in which I'd lived and peered in the windows. Everything inside was polished—the house had been domesticated. The root cellar wasn't flooding. There was a meditation room in the garage and pillows where a lathe had spun wood into bowls. There was no leaking roof and no kerosene lamps (everything had been electrified). Nothing was left of the feeling the place had once had. I looked toward the apple tree I'd successfully protested my father cutting, the one under which I'd grown up counting deer, the one I'd climbed, the one the picture window looked out on, the one that made the house a house with its treeness. There was nothing to say. Even as I held his hand, I could feel the man beside me moving away.

When I was your age, Zach, I wrote and illustrated a story about a fat pig who goes on a diet. The pig lived in a house with a hanging light bulb and ate at a table in a chair. I made a cover for the story out of cardboard and burlap I embroidered. My mother typed my words and stitched the pages to the cover and I bound its spine with a strip of yellow electrical tape. I don't remember if this was before or after I called home from the principal's office to ask if I could bring home the school hamster. My mother told me I could not, because she and my father had just bought pigs. Pigs?

I remember the battery-powered electric fence strung around the field next to our stone house, the trough my father welded, and the four pigs that greeted me when I got home from school, their breath visible in the cool autumn air. I also remember the pigs pushing the feed trough up against the electric fence, grounding it, and thereby freeing themselves to wander. Once my parents followed what they thought were the pigs' tracks all the way through our woods to Lake Iroquois, only to return to find them back in their pen waiting to be fed.

Every evening it was my job to feed Bacon, Lettuce, Tomato, and Sandwich (I don't remember who thought up these names) the leftovers my mom brought home from the lunchroom at the school for developmentally disabled kids where she taught. I loved dumping the white bucket full of stinky slop over the fence as the pigs squealed. My favorite was Lettuce. She was pink with grey blotches. When it snowed, I tried to cover her with my shrunken Hudson Bay Blanket, but she would have none of it.

Our pigs, Zach, weren't pets like your Sid. They were raised to be slaughtered. In fact, I even watched as my father pushed their heads into feed buckets and led them up the ramp into the back of his dump truck. It was just a few minutes drive to our neighbor's slaughterhouse, but as my dad was boarding up the truck bed to thwart their escape, one pig hurled its body against a board. The 2×4 went flying and hit my father between the eyes. I think of this now, Zach, because it occurs to me that Temple Grandin's calming chutes actually deny animals the opportunity to grow afraid on their way to slaughter. Her chutes hold animals tight, leaving them no chance to revolt.

When my lover (the one I'd taken to see my childhood home) left me, I was alone again in the brutal way I had been as a child. But as a child I hadn't recognized my loneliness as such. It was simply all I knew. In any case, Zach, I imagine it is loneliness (lack of love) that draws me now to Temple Grandin and to you.

Forgive me this long, rambling letter. All I really meant to say was that the cruelty of the state and its ordinances is unbearable and that I send my regards to Sid and you.

JUMAH

You've attempted suicide twelve times and now you're on another hunger strike. Strapped into a restraint chair, a feeding tube forced up your nose, down your throat, and into your stomach, you scream. Officials at Guantánamo pump you full of liquid nutrients and laxatives and keep you in the chair until you shit yourself. A soldier tells you he is sorry. You thank him. He doesn't want your thanks. He says he wants you to know that we're not all bad. Another soldier cries. *These are examples*, you write in a letter your lawyer smuggles out of Camp Delta, *to show the reader that there are some soldiers who have humanity.*

The chair in which you're lashed, Jumah, was made by someone who lives in a small town near where I live. I drive there. Is anything happening in Denison? I ask the woman behind the desk at the Budget Inn.

Not that I know of, she says, handing me a key.

It is unusually cold for early September in Iowa. I'm shivering in my thin Shut Down Guantánamo T-shirt.

I sleep in my clothes, wake at eight, check out of my room, and breakfast at the Trio Café across from Landscapes Unlimited, a cement lawn ornament store on Denison's main drag—Lincoln Highway. Inside, the walls are decorated with paintings of animals dressed in hunting caps with guns. There are papers at the counter. On the front page of the *Sioux City Journal* is a photo of Iraqis burning an effigy of the Pope. I order an English muffin and coffee.

Everyone here knows each other—it's obvious by the way they talk and joke. I pretend to read the paper, but really I'm eavesdropping. At one table, a woman talks about her mother: I tried her cell phone and she ain't answering. She's got half-timers—forgets half of what you tell her.

The other talk is of cutting hay, the price of houses, and of living in the country where you don't have to see your neighbors.

The first person I say more than a few words to in Denison is dressed in a blue vest. I meet her at Thrifty White, a drug store in the city center. No, we don't stock film, she apologizes. It expires before we can sell it and everyone shoots digital these days.

She has shockingly blue eyes and her white hair is cut short. I ask if she's lived here long.

Forty-two years.

She tells me she moved here to bury her first husband. Then she met her second one. I ask if she knows Tom Hogan, the man who made the chair in which you're presently being tortured, Jumah. He's a super guy, Jan says. Someone told me he was a general in the military! Heard him on the radio this morning talking about the rainstorm. Have you been out to his house and seen his chairs? I used to live next door to him. He should be down at the sheriff's office now. I'm sure he'll talk to you.

I exit the Thrifty White and stroll past the coming attractions window at the Reed Theater on Broadway. *The Odd Will Get Even*, the displayed movie poster reads. I continue on, stepping around a construction site and a wooden billboard announcing the birth of a new jail. At the police station, a man on the other side of a thick window buzzes me in. I climb the stairs and answer a thin woman's 'what do you want?' Minutes later, I'm shaking hands with Tom Hogan.

Jumah, the reason I'm telling you all this is the same reason I keep writing you letters that keep getting returned, some ripped open, others unread, all of the envelopes stamped *refused*: because my not writing would imply that writing doesn't matter, and I cannot stand such a thought. Even if what I write is simply a record of barbarism (as Walter Benjamin maintains *there is no cultural document that is not at the same time a record of barbarism*), it is still a record. Ultimately, though, I know the real issue is whether such records are read and responded to. Did you know, Jumah, that when asked for a nonviolent solution to WWII, Mahatma Gandhi proposed that those imprisoned in camps commit suicide to show the others outside what they claimed they couldn't see? Thereafter, George Orwell stated that such nonviolent forms of protest depend upon a sane society—a society in which people respond to what they see morally.

Gandhi is my hero. I'm a pacifist, but not always, Tom Hogan tells me. Bear with me because it's gruesome, but if I believe in my cause enough to pour gasoline over my enemy's women and children and set them on fire—because that's what war is—then I'll do it.

I sit across from him in his office above the county jail, hunched in my thick, zipped-up, hooded sweatshirt, as he winds a rubber band around his hand, then rubs it back and forth across the desk that has on it a six-inch model pig next to a piece of bullet-shattered glass. As many as 9,400 hogs are killed every day in Denison's two slaughterhouses. As a young man, Hogan worked in one of these meat packing plants.

Back then the plant where he worked was known as Farmland Foods. Now it's owned by Smithfield Foods, Inc. Smithfield is a corporation that Temple Grandin claims *could serve as a conscientious model for the entire American pork industry*. Others argue that genetically engineered hogs at Smithfield's factory farms are kept in stalls so small they cannot turn around, and that these hogs chew on stall bars, practice rooting and nest-building on concrete they imagine is straw, are covered with sores, tumors, and bruises, and often suffer from sprained and broken legs. Smithfield workers, from what I gather, aren't treated much better. Repetitive motion injuries are the most pervasive. Conditions are crowded and workers often cut themselves with knives and on machinery. Many workers labor all day in thirty-four degree slaughter rooms and receive just eight dollars an hour. It also appears that Smithfield Foods, Inc. has repeatedly denied worker compensation claims, employs a majority Latino workforce, and exploits workers' immigrant status to keep them quiet about workplace abuses. Named after what slaughterhouse workers call aggressive pigs, 'The Biting Sow Award' is Hogan's way of rewarding those who admit their petty professional mistakes. He places the pig with its one ear cocked, obscenely turned up snout, and ridiculous grin, on officers' desks whenever they confess to bending a police car fender, say, or forgetting a bulletproof vest at a crime scene. The sow recently came back to bite Hogan after he got a speeding ticket in a neighboring county this February.

Hogan is talking about what he calls 'plausible deniability.' He tells me he hopes that if he had lived next door to Auschwitz he wouldn't have ignored the suffering. I say I've come to ask him the same questions I am asking myself about the roles we play in other peoples' suffering, because I can't sit in my room fearing that people are being tortured and not do something. I'm not sure I believe in a just war, I say. I don't think I could set fire to anybody. I believe in protest. But I'm not sure it works anymore. Anyway, everyone should be allowed at least the right to protest, especially those detained at Guantánamo.

The problem is, Hogan argues, protest *does* work. Look at Gandhi. If he was alive, I bet he'd wish he hadn't done what he did. He'd want the British back there. And if Martin Luther King had lived, he would have thought, 'What did I do?!' when he saw the Watts Riots—

I disagree. I think 'those people,'—I mark the quotations in the air with my fingers—are happy to have their independence!

Ha, Hogan snorts. Then what about the Iraqis?

Do they have independence? I ask. Or an occupied country?

I think prisoners should be allowed to protest. But as soon as they're in danger, we should intervene. If those chairs did help save lives, I'm proud, Hogan says, smiling.

It all began when a colleague broke his own arm trying to restrain someone. Anytime you restrain someone there's a risk, Hogan explains.

He lists examples. When he gets to the hog tie, he acts it out for me. It's where you cuff the arms and then tuck the legs behind them like this. The hog tie can asphyxiate. So we made the chair.

We? I ask.

My wife and I. Then hospitals wanted it. I said okay. I could see the need. Then the military wanted it—

I interrupt to ask whether he'll continue to sell the chair to the military given that twenty-five of his chairs have ended up at Guantánamo. He doesn't answer. Instead, he says, Commandant Hood called me the other day and said, 'I bet you never got a call from Cuba before.' Then he told me, 'I just want to let you know we're not torturing anybody down here.' That made me feel better. I slept better that night.

Let me put it another way. If you knew absolutely that the chair was being used to torture, would you stop selling it? I ask him.

I'd like to believe I am good. We all have good and bad in us. You never know. I'm a capitalist. But I deplore torture. I think any time you demean or humiliate someone that's torture and we should uphold the Geneva Conventions, every single one. As soon as you say you can waterboard, it's a slippery slope. But you see I'm not sure how my chair's being used.

I look out the window to my left. The day has turned overcast.

In Denison's basement jail, Hogan shows me the chair. An exact replica of the one you're in now, Jumah, it sits against the block wall looking like a weight-lifting bench someone's folded in half. We walk over to it and Hogan reads me the warning rubber-banded to the chair handle, underlining each word with his finger.

Then he says, A mentally ill person told me it should have padding and be painted blue, so we changed it. She said, 'I didn't think you would listen to me because I'm mentally ill,' but I said, 'I think you're the person we should be listening to.'

A guard leads a young woman in an orange uniform into a cell directly to the left of where Hogan and I are standing. I watch as the prisoner unfolds a black blanket and wraps it around her shoulders. Have you heard of an autistic woman who designed a restraint chair like yours to calm herself? I ask Hogan.

No, I haven't, he says. Then he turns to the guard. Do you remember the prisoner who used to ask to be put in the chair? We would tell him, 'No, you have to be violent to be put in the chair,' and he'd say, 'I'll get violent then!' He would beg for it.

If you're talking about the same person I'm thinking of, I think it was a mental problem, the guard nods. He'd sit there and he'd fight it a little. Then he'd say, 'Okay, I feel better now.'

The restraint chair breaks your hunger strike, Jumah. You aren't near death. They don't force feed you to save you, even though Hogan says he designed the chair to help save lives. I study the photograph taken of you before you were detained. Dressed in a blue sweater, you hold a pencil to your mouth as you talk on the phone. I study your ruffled brown hair and averted eyes, and imagine smoking cigarettes with you in a garden and talking about books. I'm not sure why I feel close to you, close enough to imagine a correspondence. Perhaps, initially, it was seeing this photo in which you seem so like me—because this snapshot portrays the recognizable need you, too, have to communicate.

I have read your prison narrative. I have read, *As I hold my pen, my hand is shaking*; I have read of your being urinated on, Jumah, of your being made to walk barefoot on barbed wire, forced to breathe chemical odors, stripped of clothes and left naked with no pillow, no mattress, only the cold metal of a cage. I have read of petrol injected into your penis and of the time your lawyer came and you excused yourself, made a noose, and jumped from the sink in the restroom. No one, Jumah, should be shackled to the ground beneath a naked, menstruating female guard. No one. How, in the face of this, can I write to you? And of what can I write? Of the color of the sweater I am wearing—pale-green?

TOPSY

In 1903, we used electricity to put you to death after you killed three men in three years. At first it was thought that you—a ten-foot-tall, twenty-foot-long, domesticated Indian elephant—would publicly hang, but an animal rights organization protested. Hanging, they insisted, was cruel and inhumane. Electrocution had recently replaced the gallows in New York State (after a dentist proposed the idea that death by electrocution was neither cruel nor painful), so it was decided that you, too, should 'humanely' fry. First you were fed carrots poisoned with cyanide. Then you were dressed in copper shoes, covered with electrodes, and led to a special platform on Coney Island where you'd lived and performed for a number of years.

In ten seconds you were dead. One thousand five hundred people gathered to watch and Thomas Edison caught it all on film.

The most obviously devastating footage in *Mr. Death*—a documentary about Fred Leuchter, electric chair specialist and Holocaust denier—is its appropriation of Edison's short film of your electrocution. In it, you prance. There is a sense of superiority in your mammothness. Then rope-like fasteners are strung to your unsuspecting body. (On the chairs Leuchter both oversees and rebuilds, such fasteners are referred to as *non-incremental restraint systems* and are fashioned out of nylon.) Ultimately, you jerk and collapse, hide smoking.

Leuchten, in German, means to be lit or shining. *Leuchter* is a chandelier. Leuchter, the man, traveled to Auschwitz for his honeymoon and chipped samples from gas chamber walls while his wife waited for him in the car. I don't know that we ever slept in the same bed there, Leuchter's wife comments in *Mr. Death*.

Their relationship didn't last. Leuchter doesn't speak of this in the documentary, but talks instead about the electric chair and how messy it is. On the messiness of the electric chair: when Pedro Medina—a Cuban who came to Miami after Castro briefly opened the port of Mariel for emigration in 1980—was being executed in the Florida State Prison's electric chair on March 25, 1997, flames shot from his head and smoke filled the execution chamber, and he was thereafter said to have taken three deep breaths. Jay Wiechert, an electric-chair consultant from Fort Smith, Arkansas, was hired to investigate the cause of the malfunctioning chair. Wiechert identified the problem: one of the two sponges used to conduct the current had not been soaked in saline solution. Then, in July, 1999, the chair malfunctioned again and Wierchert was called back. This time he suggested that because the size of an inmate varies, the protocol calling for a specification of both volts and amps was *too technical* and needed to be rewritten. Coincidental asides: 1. In 1800, more persons were put to death in Fort Smith, Arkansas, than in any other place in North America; 2. Following the Mariel boatlift, thousands of Cubans were detained at a military training ground just outside Fort Smith. After being stripped naked, handcuffed to bunks, and tortured, the detainees rioted. Several guards were eventually charged with abuse. One guard testified that his actions may have been excessive, but that he was only encouraging a detainee to eat because he was on a hunger strike. People, he says, urinate and defecate in the chair. As urine is a conductor, his job, he argues, is to make sure the persons doing the electrocuting don't also get electrocuted.

Mr. Death plays on my computer, but I'm not watching. I am on my back on the floor of my Colonial Terrace apartment in Iowa City, studying the ceiling. Leuchter's monotone babbling is frightening: *How do I sleep at night? I sleep very well at night knowing these persons are going to have a humane execution.*

What is humane, Topsy? Is it shooting prisoners full of electricity so they can suffer less when it comes to their state-determined deaths? I think of your life—of the domesticating done to you, and I see you being led to the special platform all the more clearly. They tricked you. You thought you were performing and you pranced. I rewind *Mr. Death* to your electrocution. You are luminous. The film is silent, shot as if in a state of moral and emotional anesthesia.

It plays on.

HORIZON

When it rains in Rwanda, the road runs red. People stand close to the doors of their houses with pots at the end of outstretched arms. Today, however, there is no sign of rain. The sky is blue and cloudless.

VANISHING POINT

Back when I still carried my camera everywhere I went, as if it were a child, I drove from Kentucky to North Carolina to study William Gedney's photographs and writings. Gedney had taught at the college I'd attended but had died of AIDS-related causes a few years before I entered. He'd also lived below the poverty level

and photographed in Kentucky, just as I was then living and doing. Flipping through one of Gedney's notebooks in Durham,
I came across references to Pieter Bruegel and to Hokusai. It
appeared that these artists' extreme distance from their subjects
—they both render human figures the size of ants amidst overwhelming landscapes—moved Gedney.

But Gedney never shied away from his subjects. Nor did he
alienate them within or from their environments. Often, though,
hidden subjects appear in his works, figures who grow visible—
like a fourth child standing behind three others peeling potatoes
in a Kentucky kitchen—only after the viewer has lived with the
photographs for a while.

WIDE ANGLE

There is talk on this road, the one that leads from Kigali to
Ntarama, of its imminent paving. Houses along its edge have
been marked with a white X as they are slated for destruction.
The paved road will be wide.

HAND HELD

Duende lived in small spaces. I knew him in two: on 17th Street
in the Barrio Viejo, Tucson, and in an Ukrainian neighborhood in
Chicago. Each of these rented rooms was big enough only to turn

around in. The rooms were no longer than the length of a futon (unfolded each evening), and in each was squeezed a dresser and a few crates filled with books.

For the time that he would have it, I shrank myself into these rooms with him. Throughout the period in which he lived on 17th Street, when I wasn't in his horse-sized room, I was in my Lucky Street art studio where I showered in an industrial-sized sink and closed my ears each evening to the heavy breathing of the neighboring pyrotechnic theater troupe's fire-eaters. Whenever Duende visited me at Lucky Street, he entered stealthily. If he knocked, he waited outside, sucking his belly in as he pressed himself up against the wall to the right. When I opened the door, sensing he was near, I would spot him only after my eyes had adjusted to the dark hallway. Each time I opened the door, I, too, held my breath. What we felt for one another was surprise. Neither could believe the other existed. Hence, we felt the need to play up this surprise, to heighten its power.

JUMP CUT

There was a time when Duende imposed himself surreptitiously into my life, appearing one day in my university classroom and then accompanying me to my home where he proceeded to untie my boots. I wore steel-toed Redwings back then, and these boots were what made up Duende's mind. He loved me first for my boots, tops cut off so my calves could breathe, laces different widths. Why would an old pair of work boots entice? They spoke, I know now, of walking through ditches, forests, deserts, and of a certain endurance. (Duende and I used to disappear into the Arizona high desert together. Sometimes we buried ourselves in the dirty sand of dry river washes. Once, we watched a Gila Monster eat its fill of ants as they crawled, one by one, unwittingly up out of a hole in the sand, the monster's tongue lighting fast.)

The last time I saw Duende, he was spinning himself back through the doors of the supermarket where he worked. This movement was not unlike that first jump he took off the back bumper of my brown diesel truck. The jump was childlike—its whimsy bore itself in the air like the spore of a dandelion flower.

BLIND SPOT

In Rwanda, I am angry that I am alone and my attention wanders. When I was with Duende, I shared my eyes with him and only him. As a truck rattles past, I tell myself that I will meet the man I am to marry on this road. I will the driver to turn around, stop, pick me up and carry me off, but he disappears into a cloud of red dust.

Minutes later I meet Abraham. He overtakes me (he has been walking—as have I—since early morning, though with his long stride he has covered more ground), speaking English shyly and asking where I am headed. It turns out we know people in common and this seems miraculous to us, even though the population of Rwanda is not overwhelming and the chances of my knowing his cousin are not slim. I have heard, as well, of the baby his sister —who was sick for just three days before she died—left behind.

Abraham walks with a briefcase on top of which he's folded a dress coat, and he wears a ball cap pulled down low over his long, curling eyelashes. The shoelaces of his polished dress shoes keep coming untied, and we keep stopping so he can tie them. Where the road forks, we rest in the shade of the overhanging roof of a house colored the same rust-orange as the dirt of the road. Across the street, children shout, their voices sharp. *Muzungu! Muzungu!*

Muzungu is a marker for everything foreign and moneyed. Abraham laughs because he is indigenous to this region of Rwanda. He is here in Ntarama to attend his sister's funeral, but because his skin is as dark as those who taunt us, it is the fact that he is speaking English, a foreign tongue, and sitting with me, my pale skin sun-burnt and flaking, that makes him a foreigner and reveals his Ugandan upbringing.

Do you have a fiancé? he asks.

I will travel no farther with him today. I am taking the fork to the right. I shake my head 'no.'

I can be! Abraham says, grinning. I can be!

The church memorial at Ntarama is guarded by Delphine, a young woman who spends the day waiting for tourists. As she waits, she studies an English language dictionary. I follow her through the gates to the church, balancing on top of a wobbly wooden pew, stepping hesitantly onto another pew and then another until I've made my way over—without ever touching—a floor strewn with human bones.

In neighboring buildings are more bones. They are piled so high I have a hard time comprehending how they ever could have been bodies. Nor can I imagine how the rags that hang from rafters were once shirts, trousers, dresses. Pots, thermoses, and necklaces are the only other relics. Some shoes. Much of the slab of granite near the mass graves is blank. It shines smooth and black in the sun. No list exists of the names of the dead buried here. Whoever they were, there were no papers found on their bodies. Just as there was no one, by the time the pits were dug, left alive who could identify them.

AVOIDANCE OF EYE CONTACT

Abraham's face looks oddly pinched sitting across from me at the house in which I stay with its concrete floors and iron window bars. He sits to my right at the wood table the color of honey. He has come, on his way back to Kigali, to ask me for money.

I have two sons, he says. It seems hard for him to confess this. I was married, he continues, to a Ugandan woman. She wouldn't come to Rwanda with me. She wanted to stay on her land.

Abraham confesses he loved this woman so much that when he left her he suffered from ulcers. Fellow soldiers jeered him. You're feeling this way because of a woman?

I tell him I will do what I can to find a sponsor to pay for his children's school fees. Then I walk him up to the school room I am helping construct. It is half built. Each brick has been hand-made and ferried to the site on shoulders. Abraham says that a building is a good investment because it will always be there, whereas a car breaks down and costs to maintain. I do not tell him that I have no house back home, only a car, and that the road still calls, even though I dream of settling down.

FORCED PERSPECTIVE

I have played the man-I-will-marry-game for the past ten years. It started when I was manning a country store in Blackey, Kentucky, and helping care for the eighty-year-old proprietor, Joe Begley, whose emphysema had flared. Joe and his wife Gay had taken me under their wing when I'd first arrived in the region to work for the weekly paper. They were a couple famous for their anti-strip mining activism and the store was a meeting place for activists and community members concerned about their land.

I was standing in Gay's place behind the counter—the walls and ceiling filled every which way with items Joe and Gay had collected, from hard hats to old spinning wheels to political posters—when a poet entered the dark store, crossed its coffee-colored floorboards, and introduced himself.

He and I wrote letters for a time. I thought we were fated. Then his letters grew scarce and finally stopped arriving all together. I found myself that fall walking up to the strip mine behind the cabin I was then renting and staring down at the gigantic swimming-pool-sized hole in which piles of gravel, coal, and dirt had been stockpiled by bulldozers. It was difficult to understand, while perched on the edge of this abyss, that I was gazing into the inside of the earth. Perspective played tricks. The mine took on the guise of a horizon. A Renaissance painter sketching the scene would have had trouble establishing a vanishing point, for beyond the strip job was a forest, and above the forest, a towering mountain.

THE GAZE

There is a book I like very much that documents Max Sebald's walk around East Anglia, England, as he contemplates all that was kept secret from him throughout his German childhood. In this book, Sebald unearths whatever is to be unearthed from the English countryside that has to do, however remotely, with the Holocaust. Throughout, Sebald is also obsessed with 'the gaze.' Mentions of blind spots, avoidance of eye contact, staring, falsification of perspective, and spectacles (in which one is both actor and audience) dot the manuscript, as does mention of animal life in the form of silkworms, pheasants, peacocks, quail, herring, and fantastical beasts. Looking at the other, whether animal or human, Sebald hints, is impossibly complex, predicated on a human need to establish patterns and various other ways of seeing. Yet haunted as he was by his Nazi heritage, Sebald knew that one is never free to only observe. One is always also acting.

Six years ago, I wrote Sebald a letter. Outside the envelope, on top of the folded flap, I pasted a drawing of a dog copied from Diego Velasquez's *Las Meninas* painting. Reading Sebald had reminded me of Velasquez's painting himself painting this stuffy court scene, and thereby inspiring other artists to question their own places in the world. The letter itself was a plea requesting funding, as I had been accepted to study at the university where Sebald was tenured, but I couldn't afford the tuition. Sebald, responding to what he called my 'most unusual' letter, kindly explained there were no scholarships available.

The following year, he was killed in an accident on an English byway and I bemoaned all over again my missed chance to have been his student.

I don't know much about Sebald's life. I do know, though, that he is survived by a wife and daughter, and that he didn't keep a computer in his office, liked to travel lightly with just a rucksack and a small automatic camera, and thought the photographs accompanying his texts should be as grainy as the type.

I've seen just two photographs of him. In one he sits in front of a shadowy painting of a boy's head. In the other he is again in front of a painting—a darkly speckled canvas I keep mistaking for a coal mine. There are spectacles in his hands. (He must have taken them off for the photo.) His mustache widens his long face. When I invite him out of the mine in which he is trapped, he only looks at me, shining his lantern-like eyes into mine. His face is splattered with mud. I hand him a kerchief. He takes it, wipes his face, and then puts his eyeglasses on, his back bent at the same angle as the height of the mine, his galoshes knee-high. He gestures to me. I crawl after him. His arm flies up. I stop. Gaseous tight air burns the top of my esophagus. There's a deer in front of us.

VIEW OF A SUGAR CANE FIELD

Fog weaves through banana tree leaves as men push bicycles loaded with yellow jerry cans uphill. The road winds, plateauing above a sugar cane field on the other side of the hill. Dugouts float in the river and storks rest in tall trees that line the field below. The view reminds me of Brueghel's hunters skirting an outcrop, villagers skating below.

I am on my way to Kigali as Abraham wants to give me a tour of the city. I walk quickly. Girls traipse barefoot out of the cane fields. I catch up to them just as one happens upon a small fish by the roadside. She bends regally—as a load of brush is balanced on her head—and picks up the blue-black dead thing. It is halved, the size of her thumb. She squeezes it, making a face as guts trail out its cut end.

For how long have you been carrying these bundled faggots?

For as long as we remember.

And what of the snakes in the sugar cane?

We aren't afraid of them, sir.

In death one becomes fluent in all languages. Sebald is just one of the dead walking among these girls.

Abraham and I circumnavigate the city's perimeter at a fast clip. We walk past hand-painted ads. These ads communicate—beyond what they're here to sell—a proud whole, rather than a mechanized, fractured self. One ad is for mattresses and features the painted figure of a woman near a bed. Another is simply painted text on a stucco storefront: *Black and Lovely. Time to Get Lovely.* The ads are beautiful and make me want to believe in human resiliency. But then Abraham directs my attention back to the road, telling me it divides the rich from the poor, and farther along, the Muslim sector from the Christian.

We walk on to the university where I am to meet a friend. We are early, my friend nowhere in sight. A cap vender weaves his way toward us and Abraham gladly surveys the caps on the rotational hanger the vender dangles. The prettiest cap in Abraham's eyes has a McDonald's label on it. I explain the meaning of the symbol and Abraham waves the vender on. An old woman approaches, eyes cloudy, walk bent. She speaks with Abraham and he unfurls for her a 100 franc note. She is drunk on medicine, he tells me. Because of the genocide.

Abraham, too, suffers from war memories. He was part of the Ugandan-reared Tutsis, who drove the genocidal Hutus out of the country. He fought, as well, in the Rwandan-perpetrated genocide in the Democratic Republic Congo and in Angola. He was recently asked to be part of the peace-keeping effort in Darfur, but opted to study computers instead. Why didn't he refuse to fight back when he was just seventeen? He could have. Others he knew in Uganda refused to, he says. However, his parents, elite Tutsis who had sought exile in Uganda during the 1959 Hutu revolutionary rampage, had drilled it into his head that Rwanda was his country (though, at that time, he had never set foot here) and that it was his duty to fight for the family's right to return. Abraham says he can't believe he is still in one piece. He isn't missing an arm, a leg, his blood hasn't been infected with AIDS. He is thin and straight as a piece of sugar cane. Beside him, I wish for some cane to chew—for the sweet, crunchy pith protected by the rough, outer stalk. It takes work to whittle one's way to sweetness, but the sun is strong and I'm thirsty.

When Abraham asks whether Africans and Americans can marry in the United States, I pretend not to hear. I've given up on my friend's arrival and I propose that Abraham and I walk back to where I am staying.

I always sang when I walked when I was fighting, Abraham tells me. It's what saved me. Do you sing?

We are walking across a dip in the landscape, the red of the road omnipresent, the dust, *ivumbi*, everywhere in the air, in the corners of our eyes, our hair. Abraham says it is harder to part with someone with whom you've had children, and I am arguing. It is hard to part, even when you haven't.

Abraham will write to me months later about seeing—on a website on which I've posted a request for sponsors for his children's schooling—personal advertisements written by African-American women. *It's interesting*, he will email, *but I feel I've given up on marrying after experiencing much rejection by my first girlfriend and all my love and compassion towards women has been ruined by the genocide.*

I will then concede that Abraham's broken heart is much more broken than mine. There is, of course, no comparison.

CONGOLESE TRADITIONAL SCULPTURE

Matisse purchased a small African sculpture—now known to be an *nkisi*—from the Congo in 1906. Picasso saw it and was so blown away that he began visiting African collections in various museums and the following year produced *Les Demoiselles d'Avignon*, a painting of women with mask-like faces to which the birth of Cubism is now attributed.

Usually carved in the shape of human beings, *minkisi* (the Ki-Kongo plural of *nkisi*) sculptures were first created near the

NOTE: The nation-state I term 'Congo' in this essay has been known since colonial times as Congo Free State, Belgian Congo, Congo-Leopoldville, Congo-Kinshasa, Zaire, and Democratic Republic of the Congo.

mouth of the Congo River in the seventeenth century. Each *nkisi* was the work of a sculptor (who carved the figure from the *Canarium schweinfurthii* tree, the roots and leaves of which were traditionally used to treat fever, malaria, and infections) as well as a *nganga* or medicine man. After the sculptor finished the carving, the *nganga* was called upon to stuff the *nkisi* (in cavities cut into the figure's belly) with white clay, dirt from graves, bones, herbs, and other substances with evocative names (such as *kalazima*, or charcoal—its KiKongo name sounding like *zima*, 'that it may strike or extinguish'). The *nganga* was also paid to adorn the sculpture with feathers, beads, buttons, and mirrors, and to accord it its own particular songs and rituals to invoke certain spirit powers. After this, the *nkisi* was thought potent enough to inflict death or disease on enemies, or to cure or protect the innocent. *Minkisi* were also used in traditional judicial systems. Suspected criminals took oaths in front of the sculptures and thereafter tested the truth of their words by driving nails (each nail was considered a *mambu* or 'word') into the *minkisi*. They were then required to extract their driven nails out of the wooden sculptures. If anyone failed, he or she was deemed guilty.

Between 1885 and 1921 (when a *nkisi* could be bought for a yard of calico, but the charge of activating it by a *nganga* was fifty yards of calico or the price of a slave), Portuguese, French, Belgian and Arab powers began fighting for control of the Congo, capturing *minkisi* as they warred. These colonists hoarded and locked up the *minkisi*, afraid of these *devil-like, rudely-carved scarecrows* considered synonymous with Congolese resilience and believed to be powerful enough to relieve slaves' sufferings. By 1921, the last of the *banganga* (the KiKongo plural of *nganga*) to survive the Europeans' witch hunts were said to have surrendered their *minkisi* after Congolese prophet Simon Kimbagu (who preached that God was black) converted them and thousands more to Christianity.

Born in 1947, Tshibumba Kanda grew up to become one of a number of genre painters in the Katanga region whose repertoire of paintings are based primarily on popularized memories of colonial Congolese history. But Tshibumba's most famous work —a series of 102 paintings, *The History of Zaire*—was created outside the traditional "Temps Colonial" repertoire. Under the urging of Johannes Fabian, a North American-educated anthropologist, Tshibumba not only painted *The History of Zaire* series, he related an oral history (which Fabian recorded) of the Congo that begins with the loss of ancestral stories and the colonization of the Congolese by Belgian King Leopold. *There was no way out. We lived in slavery. Our sovereignty died right there,* Tshibumba says of the moment Leopold weaseled power away from Congolese ruler Banza Kongo.

Tshibumba's ancient scenes are set amidst lush landscapes

and painted from culturally inherited memories. Of course, colo- ·
nial European influence infiltrates these memories, just as the act
of painting itself is trapped within European tradition and discourse. But Tshibumba explains, *As regards painting—of course we
know that the Europeans brought painting. So in the end, I'm following an idea of the whites when I paint. But when we paint, we depict
matters that concern us and that we have seen.*

Tshibumba's ancient scenes in *The History of Zaire* series
share visual qualities with early African figurative sculpture and
Cubist art. His representations of twentieth century Congolese
struggles for independence, on the other hand, embrace a more
photorealist view—the perspective is less Cubist and the treat-
ment of the figure (especially that of leader Patrice Lumumba)
more 'realistic.' He returns, though, to the powerful sculpture-in-
spired folk-style when rendering his visions of future events. And
decades later, these paintings—in which people of varying ages
walk aimlessly and men march stone-faced in uniform—portray
precisely today's Congolese reality.

*We will rise up against each other . . . I think there will be big trou-
ble,* Tshibumba told Fabian, speaking about what he thought
would occur at the end of Mobutu's reign. As he predicted, following the 1994 Rwandan genocide which left just under a million dead, Rwanda's Patriotic Front (RPF) chased genocide perpetrators and other refugees into the Congo, overthrew Mobutu,
who was sheltering the perpetrators, and helped their ally Lau-
rent Kabila into power. Upon assuming the Congolese presi-

dency, however, Kabila surprised everyone by inviting the Rwandan genocide perpetrators (whom he had just helped the RPF fight) into the new Congolese army. The RPF then reinvaded the Congo, and by the end of 1998 the toll of the war had reached four million.

It is believed that Tshibumba was among those killed in Congolese genocide. A victim of the future he prophesied, Tshibumba's paintings are the remains of his unique view: each paint stroke is a nail, a word, a life.

Let no one do away with my monument! Let my statue stand . . .
Whosoever . . . shall set his own name on the statue . . . saying 'It is my
statue,' or shows it to an outsider and says, 'Erase it and set my name
(there-on),' may . . . all the great gods lay on him a terrible curse.

"COMMEMORATIVE INSCRIPTION" COPIED BY AN

OLD BABYLONIAN SCHOLAR FROM A NOW-MISSING

STONE MONUMENT IN A TEMPLE AT UR

3 0 0 0 B C

Tin and copper collide in fire, birthing bronze on land between
the Tigris and Euphrates rivers. Neither ore is native to the region. Tin from northeasterly mountains arrives on the backs of
donkeys. Ships bring copper from southern climes up the Persian
Gulf. The need for strong and durable bronze spurs not only
trade, but warfare. Armies, outfitted with bronze weapons and armor, protect the mines and guard the arrival of tin caravans and
copper shipments.

Far away, the tin and copper mines are small—some just two
feet wide. Teenagers mine the ore, working on their bellies and
burrowing as far as two miles underground to chip away at rock

they heat with fire and then crack with cool water. Mining-related injuries and illnesses are common. When a miner dies, the burial hole is already dug. Skeletal remains litter the mines.

The smelting of each pound of copper requires the felling and charring of four century-old trees. Demand for millions of tons of smelted copper over several centuries results in severe deforestation. Gilgamesh, a king who rules harshly and sleeps with other men's wives, inhabits a garden near the Tigris and Euphrates fork. He and his friend, Enkidu, kill the guardian of the cedar forest. But, as the guardian prophesied, thereafter Enkidu grows sick and dies. Thousands of years later, a scholar will theorize that the *Epic of Gilgamesh* is nothing less than a documentation of the shortage of wood in Mesopotamia. In fact, he will claim, Gilgamesh *has the typical logger mentality: cut it down, and never mind the consequences.*

Someone abandons a baby in a cradle of reeds on the Euphrates. Reared by a gardener, this infant, Sargon, grows up to become a royal cup-bearer. One night he dreams of the ruler drowning in a river of blood. Upon hearing of the dream, the ruler tells his chief smith to throw Sargon into a mold and smelt him like a bronze statue. But Sargon wages war against the ruler, and in turn becomes King. As King, he builds a library of thousands of clay tablets as well as fortresses at strategic points along the Tin Road. His army of 5,400 men lives off taxes collected from conquered farmers. Responding to a need for bronze, he expands his empire westward. In a foundry somewhere in this kingdom, a bronze head modeled after Sargon (or some say his grandson Naram-Sim) is cast, eyes aglitter with precious stones.

1750 BC

The death penalty greets any captured, unauthorized feller of Mesopotamian trees.

1200 BC

The sudden unavailability of tin begets the use of iron ore. Weaker than bronze, iron requires more fuel and significantly more labor to work, until someone combines iron with charcoal and discovers a cheaper, more effective metal—steel.

150 BC

The result of Greek occupation of Mesopotamia: a bronze cast of Heracles that does not adhere to the golden rules. Heracles no longer leans on a club; his left hand is on his hip (rather than behind it), and he does not look down.

1258 AD

An army of Holagy, grandson of Genghis Khan, razes Medina al-Salaam ('City of Peace,' soon to be renamed Baghdad), slaughtering between one and two million inhabitants. Khan's Mogol army occupies the region. Gold and silver inlays, hammered into bronze, bear the influence of an ornate new visual language brought to the region by the Mongols.

1975 AD

A construction worker pulls a massive, hollow-cast, copper-alloy statue of a nude male, upper half missing, from a ditch in northern Iraq. The cuneiform text inscribed in the statue's base proclaims it to be a sculpture of Sargon's grandson Naram-Sin.

1999 AD

Scientists discover copper contamination—windblown dust from objects smelted during the Bronze Age—in a 7,000-year-old layer of ice in Greenland's glacial caps.

2003 AD

A five-person team packs the National Museum at Baghdad's immovable sculptures in sand bags and foam, and relocates another 8,000-plus movable objects to a secret bunker. In April, as U.S. missiles rain on Baghdad, looters scavenge the museum. Someone drags the bronze sculpture of Naram-Sin (the one previously found in a ditch) from an upper floor down the museum's marble steps, gouging them. On the street, at a local market, a buyer pays $300 for the sculpture, then drops it into a shit-hole for safekeeping.

2004 AD

On Baghdad's streets, Iraqi sculptor Khaled Izzat purchases sculptures of his that have been plundered from the National Museum.

I felt nothing, he says, when interviewed about watching U.S. troops tear down his forty-foot statue of Saddam Hussein. *I expected that when the regime changed, these statues would be brought down. But I thought they would put them in a museum.*

Across town, outside one of Hussein's palaces, explosives tear apart another Iraqi sculptor's two bronze statues of Hussein on horseback. The U.S. Army cleans up the site and then hands all the bombed bronze pieces back to their creator. Khalid Alussy spends several months smelting and refashioning the bronze bits into the likeness of a North American soldier bent in mourning over the boots of a fallen troop-mate. Later it is requested that he add a young Iraqi girl to the tableau. The girl's hand is to rest, comfortingly, on the mourning soldier's shoulder. The finished scene will decorate the palace exterior, in place of the Husseins.

America was never America to me. LANGSTON HUGHES

George Orwell once wrote of the hanging of a *small brown man* who steps to avoid a puddle on his way to the gallows and is bum-rushed by a dog. The dog laps the brown man's face, and the brown man, just as he is about to be hanged, shouts, *Ram! Ram! Ram! Ram!* Then a hush comes, and Orwell and the crowd walk away. Whiskey, it seems, is all these men, laughing garrulously, need.

Tonight I wish for whiskey as I watch the secretly shot cell phone video of Saddam Hussein's hanging. Here Hussein is, in front of me, facing death without a black bag. Beside him, other men, who have disguised themselves in ski masks, fix him never to come back. I don't see him fall—just the trap door beneath the gallows swinging. It isn't until I watch again that I see the blur and remember his forty-foot statue in Baghdad falling, an American flag knotted around its neck.

—

Some would ignore race, insist the effect is that of gravity, and concentrate on the mandrake, a mystical plant said to spring up at the base of a gallows, the alleged possession of which was enough to make a woman a witch during the Inquisition—a plant said to shriek as it was pulled from the ground. But not much has changed since the eighteenth century. Punishment is still a spectacle a brutish state employs mostly upon people of color to reactivate its power, and I am, murderously, still a white woman scrambling—like eighteenth century European women scrambled—to the gallows to be empowered. Whereas women back then touched the dead to be made fertile, I reach out to touch this particular martyr with my pen.

'Whiteness remains the support of writing, and it constitutes its margins, but the poem is composed of the absent blacks—you may say the deads...' Thus one may compare the written page to the white ground with black skeletons. Breyten Breytenbach quoting Jean Genet

—

Sentenced to death for the murder (in retaliation for an assassination attempt made on him while rallying support for Iraq's war against Iran) of 148 of his own countrymen (several of whom he first tortured at Abu Ghraib), Hussein was hanged at the end of a long trial during which three defense lawyers were killed, and judges, one after another, dismissed, until finally a judge was found who could get the job done—the verdict, of course, *pre-judged by the Bush aministration and its Iraqi allies.* Dahr Jamail

‒

The video removes this hanging from time, space.

... the dead live in a timeless moment ... John Berger

Concepts of time and space supposedly start to break at 10^{-43} second. In other words, time and space are approximate concepts that lose their identities when shrunk. Could this phenomenon be related to the way light freezes time when cameras slice it?

What I realize looking at the hanging video: my body can't see what it does not know. But I'm not even sure of this, or of these words, or the attempt to render anything. I follow the bouncing camera with seasick eyes. How many times can one rehash an image when it isn't an image? It's a hanging. It *happened.*

When asked whether he watched the video of the execution, one North American white man with considerable economic and political power said, *Somebody showed me parts of it. Yeah. I didn't wanna watch the whole thing ... I just, I wasn't sure what to antici-*

pate beyond the yelling and stuff like that. And I didn't ... President
George Bush

Of course he knew the hanging was a spectacle at which men
had been hired to heckle. He was deliberately misrepresenting it
to the Western press. In other words, as—it has been written before—*in most lynchings, the guilt of the victim had not been proven
in the court of law. As in most lynchings, a member of the crowd wore
a mask ... And as in most lynchings, the white press and public expressed its solidarity in the name of white supremacy and ignored any
information that contradicted the people's verdict.* Leon F. Litwack

Defense attorney Ramsey Clark on Saddam's wish just hours before he was put to death: *He wanted to read a poem, he wanted to re-
itterate you cannot plead for mercy, only truth and justice.*

—

I think of the man in Florida who was told on his forty-fourth
birthday that his Marine son had been killed in a hail of gunfire in
Iraq. This man felt so guilty for not having talked his son out of
going to war that he grabbed a five-gallon can of gasoline, a pro-
pane torch, and a sledgehammer from his garage, smashed a Marine van window and began beating the dashboard, the seats, the
roof, and still his son was gone, so he poured gasoline everywhere
until the fumes he breathed were the same fumes his son took in
crossing the desert into Iraq in a tank. Then the man lit a match.

I lit a candle and placed it in my window the evening I came home from watching the 2003 late March bombing of Baghdad on a friend's TV. Biking home across the dry arroyo, I'd thought, 'This dip is more than I can ride through, coast past.' One candle lit in solidarity with other candles flickering around the world in protest of a growing fire of exploded pipe lines, a city engulfed in voluminous, toxic clouds.

—

Millions of Iraqis dead in just a few years by our own hands compared to a fraction of this number dead in twenty-four years under Hussein's thumb. This includes not only the Gulf War but the U.S.-sponsored UN sanction regime that, according to William James Martin, claimed the lives of 5,000 children and 7,500 people per month over a twelve-year period. These sanctions, Martin maintains, transformed a nation with a burgeoning middle class and with a free education and health care system (which reached ninety-three percent of the Iraqi people) into one in which most of the deaths occurring were preventable, as neither proper medicine nor clean water were available in adequate supply. And during Hussein's reign, the U.S. was his ally. In fact, during the Iran–Iraq war, Washington armed both countries and issued approval for Iraq's chemical-attack of Kurdish Halabja—the largest scale chemical weapons attack against a civilian population in history.

Not only this, Iraq's interim government (which was, of course, set up with help by the U.S.) revived capital punishment in 2005 for violent crimes.

—

He would be a lion even when caged, Little Saddam said of her
father.

Known to the Western press to have her father's temper, and
described in one news article as, *tall, slim and blonde, a well-turned
out society woman, dressing in the latest styles,* Saddam's daughter huddled on the floor of a small car toward the beginning of
the 'war on terror' as U.S. missiles fell, a gun between her feet.
Currently in exile, this mother of five survives her husband
(killed by Iraqi security officers for leaking secrets about Iraq's
nuclear program to UN inspectors), her two brothers (killed in a
six-hour American operation of gunfire and rockets), and now her
father.

Despite Little Saddam's wish to have her father temporarily
buried in Yemen *until Iraq is liberated*—in other words, free from
U.S. military domination and aggression—the lion lies buried in
an Iraqi garden.

—

What keeps me near the green screen staring at the industrial steel
of the swinging trap doors? The corrugated pattern matches that
of the footrests of Guantánamo's restraint chairs.

—

I want to be unframed by the violence around me.

... *being lynched by eyes.* Hilton Als

War as a succession of special effects. The war became film before it was shot ... Trinh T. Minh-ha

It is true. People go to porn sites now, like they used to collect postcards of lynchings, to watch beheading videos leaked from this war. Watching the rush, the plunge, the almost invisible departure, I am no better than those who watch for pleasure or who do not watch at all. It is not my neck that audibly cracks. I am simply another guilty bystander watching a brown man's toes point downward.

—

Ramsey Clark again: ... *the lesson is that you either submit or you resist, but if you resist and fail, you're dead.*

—

In Saddam Hussein's case, his neck split open.

Judicial hanging was perfected by William Marwood, who, in 1874, figured out how to drop another man so as to break his neck.

To this day it is important that the equation for judicial hangings be figured correctly, for a less immediate death by strangulation occurs if a neck isn't snapped, and if the force of the drop is underestimated, death by decapitation can follow.

Roughly two weeks after the 2006 hanging in Baghdad of the brown man with the grey beard—the one who went to the gallows unhooded, looked at one of his hecklers and asked, 'Heya hay il marjala?' ('Is this your manhood?')—, his half-brother was led to the same gallows.

Executioners placed a hood on the half-brother's head before fitting him with the noose. Then he was let fall. Immediately the rope flew back up, the noose an empty circle of air. Seeing this, the prosecutor shouted, He's escaped the noose, go down and look for him!

Silent video clips of this hanging exist, but no footage has been publically released. I imagine you know but have not seen (and does it matter that you have no visual aid, no map?) what was found there beneath the trap door.

The night delivers its screams. I squat and look at the moon. I am
tired of feeling barren, tired of loneliness and its deathly aura. I
have a book, not a baby. Some women vow to write their first book
before their first baby, but my book exists, it seems, instead of (or
at least calls attention to the absence of) a child and hence feels
like a poor reproduction. But it is not this simple. I recently refused a man who wished to father a child with me. I refused and
so it is unfair of me to compare books to babies. Especially in light
of the conversation I had with a friend (a Buddhist practitioner
in search of something 'higher' than language, not something
'lower,' like a baby) who suggested that syllables and characters
are pure, but as soon as these sounds or inscriptions are placed in
such a way as to stand for something else and become representations, they then lose their purity. Feeling defensive, I argued for
a purity that exists in language *as* representation, and was sur-

prised to find myself defending the idea of procreating metaphorically.

I suppose my argument illuminates the fact that most of the time I feel language is all I have, even though it's rarely able to approximate being. But when it does, I free-fall—until something breaks the spell (a longing for a *real* cry?) and all I am left with are a pile of letters (once upon a time scribed by feather).

—

The day my book of poetry, *Benjamin's Spectacles*, arrived, I opened the box containing my brand new author copies alone at a picnic table at the wildlife refuge where Cypress, a barred owl, is kept caged because of a lost wing. When Cypress blinks, it's like her eyelids are windshield wipers that sweep down from a central location up high. I wanted the opening of the box to be like the old days, when, as a child, I would walk the mile-long dirt road with grass growing up the middle to the mailbox, check the mail, and then slowly retrace my steps, waiting until I reached the front field with its rusting farm equipment to open any letter.

—

When words vanish, are they stuck somewhere, roadside, perhaps behind a curb? Under a pebble? Sometimes I think when they don't come and I'm waiting at my desk that they are hiding beneath a blanket of depression that hangs lop-sidedly over me.

Long ago I had a pink blanket with a satin edge. And a pink sweater, knitted by the woman I called Mama Heart, so big it came to my knees. Today I wear a ball cap and a white T-shirt and find comfort in my yellow cup with the dragon on it. The cup's lip is chipped, like a tooth, but the cup is still dreamlike in its design, its color. There is also, on this cup, a painted pheasant. It speaks a language no one knows, rendered in a cartoon-cloud full of dots —like the language animals spoke in ancient Mayan codices.

I turn to Leslie Marmon Silko's *Yellow Woman and a Beauty of the Spirit* remembering her mention of these codices. On the book's cover is an old photograph of a woman wrapped in a blanket and on her back is a child in a wood-framed papoose. On the book's back cover, the caption for the photo reads, *Memories of the Long Walk*. I think of forced marches, diseased blankets, the history of this land before I stood here. The codices, writes Silko, were pictographs and phonetic symbols painted on animal skin or agave bark paper. After a universe of gods had been created through *the coupling of the brush to the bark paper,* the codices were fed sacrificial blood.

—

Yesterday, taking pictures, trying to write an essay in images rather than words, I heard the call of a barred owl. It came from a region of the woods far away from the wounded birds' cages. It wasn't Cypress.

Later in the evening, I read notes Walter Benjamin took while his son was learning to talk. The reading comforted. I kept on, searching for that language of dots in clouds. The words Benjamin's son, Steffe, used were replacements, sound-like words that missed their exact pronunciations, yet could be easily understood —like *schringen* for *springen*, *Tetezin* for *Medizin*, *Wursität* for *Universität*, *Poffeln* for *Kortoffeln*, *Bug* for *Buch*, *Margarine* for *Mandarine*, *Smeckerling* for *Schmetterling*, *Melomodie* for *Melodie*, *Krokodilsuppe* for *Dillsuppe*, and so on.

—

What's a quote of a quote? a friend's son asked at one of my *Benjamin's Spectacles* readings, after I'd spoken about how I quote from Walter Benjamin's book of quotes, *The Arcades*, in my book.

I didn't know enough then to say what I've since determined would have been the best reply: Why, a quote of a quote is a twice intensified return to words that have been broken from their original contexts! Pulled that far out from where they originally belonged, a quote of a quote is a kind of stretch-marked language. Have you seen those lines on your mother's stomach? It is like that certain proof of passage.

Instead, I fumbled on stage, taken aback by such a real question.

—

I was addressing a poetry class at the University of Arizona. Across from me sat a young man in an owl T-shirt. After the class ended and students were gathering their things, I complimented the man on his shirt. I work with owls, he said.

I questioned him about Cypress, about the clicking sound she always makes whenever I approach her cage.

Is she imprinted—do you know if she was raised in captivity or in the wild? he asked.

I told him she was injured.

She's imprinted, he said. It's a traumatic response. She's making the noise a baby owl makes when it's hungry and asking for food from its parents.

Then a student named Carina approached me, wanting to know about my work with Sudanese refugees. I told her a little about my experience. She said she was friends with a refugee named Bior. Well, really, she said, he's my sister's friend. My sister's anorexic.

Did you know that I was too? I asked.

When I read your book I kept thinking of my sister—

There were tears in Carina's eyes. We were being pushed out of the room by an incoming class, so we made our way downstairs and seated ourselves on a red couch. Carina smoothed her skirt with her hands as she explained that Bior was a sitter for her sister. Do you know what a sitter is? she asked. It's when someone's in the hospital and needs to be watched, either so they don't throw up or try to commit suicide. Bior spends the entire night in the dark keeping a vigil. Fleeing the war in Sudan, he ate mud, lost his family, his country. How ironic, my mom says, that he is the one watching over her daughter who has everything: food, opportunity.

—

Alain Renais filmed not only *Night and Fog,* but Marguerite Duras's *Hiroshima Mon Amour.* I have seen both films numerous times. Tonight I'm watching *Night and Fog* again. As the camera pans the crematoria ovens, the journal Duras kept while waiting for her husband to return from the prison camps haunts me—especially her words about her husband's tears, after he's been rescued and returned, as the doctor proclaims his stomach too small to handle more than one morsel.

—

If Benjamin, whose death remains inseparable from the Holocaust, inhabited the age of mechanical reproduction, an age in which art and writing were becoming less esoteric and ritualistic and more political and available to a larger public, but simultaneously ever more endangered by fascist co-opting, I embody the age of virtual reproduction, an age not so different from Benjamin's, except that today's dissemination of cultural products happens more rapidly and is more far-reaching, and the language that must be wrested back from military and capitalist co-opting is no longer German, but English. Mine is an age in which, arguably, it is most responsible to birth neither book nor baby. It is an age in which we are alienated not just from our work, but from almost everything, not excluding the environment around us, our friends, families, and selves.

—

Tomaz Šalamun speaks of a Slovenian genius with a photographic memory who could perfectly recall any poem after hearing it just once, and who, after hearing someone read Blake in English, could translate the verses he'd just heard into the Slovenian language on the spot. This genius, Šalamun says, committed a strange kind of suicide. He stopped going outside, because he didn't want to kill a bug, and then he stopped eating. No one, Šalamun claims, was able to help him.

—

Benjamin's Steffe says he was a bird before he was Steffe, and that his mother-bird, with her sharp cries, scared off the bad boys who were frightening him.

Despite, or perhaps because of, what I know about this virtual age, I have an ache for this boy who exists for me only as a voice.

The bass of a pop song throbs in the apartment next door. I get up and knock on the wall. I've spent the morning reading about uranium research and the development of the bomb that was dropped on Hiroshima—the radiation of which caused thirty percent of Japanese survivors to be diagnosed and suffer from myeloid leukemia, an incurable cancer. I'm writing an academic paper on a famous author's use of uranium as an alluded-to subject, but I think the reason I'm so engrossed in the material is because my father, who never went to war, has a closely-related but extremely rare leukemia called multiple myeloma which is also found in Hiroshima survivors and is linked, among other things, to exposure to radiation.

—

It has been argued that the bombing of Japan saved lives and caused World War II to end. Such an argument, however, blatantly disregards the fact that shortly before the bombing of Hiroshima, Emperor Hirohito attempted to mediate a negotiated surrender. Sixty-three years have passed since then. Before I began reading about the atom bomb, I had assumed that at least several of those people most directly responsible for the bomb's development or deployment would have killed themselves, unable to live with their guilt after learning the horror the bomb wreaked. But not a single perpetrator, as far as I can tell from my research, did.

It might seem extreme that I should imagine suicide as a moral answer to assuming responsibility for having made and dropped the atom bomb, but I cannot stomach atrocities committed in my name. I currently feel implicated in the deaths caused by this 'war on terror' and the illegal detainment and torture at Abu Ghraib, Guantánamo, and other 'black sites' around the world. Last fall I even contemplated undertaking a hunger-strike in which I would fast to the end in protest. The fact I did not undergo the strike, and that my dissent is still locked away, barely visible, only serves to make me feel more ashamed.

—

How is it that those of us who are guilty of genocide don't kill ourselves out of devastation, but so often the survivors of genocides do? Kenzaburo Oe—who lived through the war as a boy on the

Japanese island of Shikoku, and who first visited Hiroshima to measure the decadence of his own personal suffering *by the yardstick of Hiroshima and its people*—writes of Hiroshima survivors who, upon seeing *myeloid leukemia* written on their medical charts, commit suicide. Musing that if he, too, were to be stricken with cancer he might take his own life, Oe admits that he regains courage when he meets or learns of those who have not killed themselves despite their misery—even though he suspects that these victims' stoic endurance assuages the guilt in those who master-minded and dropped the bomb.

—

Snow cakes onto the roofs of the apartments across from mine and icicles hang from the eaves above my windows. I make a tea and scuttle back to my room. I am a hostage here—my truck not starting. My father says old vehicles like mine just don't start on cold days as their motors lack sufficient compression.

By night fall, I begin to suspect I am sick like my father. There are no symptoms; I just fear that I will grow sick out of sympathy. Agha Shahid Ali, one of my favorite poets, contracted cancer of the brain five years after his mother died of the same. I am suddenly overcome with the need to check out Ali's books again from the library.

—

Near the end of the cold war, the Pentagon developed a use for all the depleted uranium waste being produced from nuclear power plants and in 1991 fired 320 tons of this waste on Iraq, and then twelve years later dumped another seventy-five tons there. Depleted uranium is nearly twice as dense as lead and leaves in its wake radioactive dust with a half-life of 4.5 billion years. This dust has increased the rates of those suffering from cancer in Iraq by at least 700 percent, and birth deformities are up 400 percent. Following the first Gulf War, thirty percent of Iraqis—the same percentage as that of Hiroshima survivors—were living with cancer. In Basra today, doctors are finding patients suffering from double and triple cancers and leukemia—once unheard of in patients below the age of twelve—in many Iraqi children.

There is, I've read, little being done to clean this radioactive dust up. Douglas Rokke, a military member in charge of the first Gulf War clean up, states that in order to clean any radioactive waste site effectively, the site must be packaged up *like a Hershey's kiss*. Rokke says that it took a $4 million facility in Barnwall, South Carolina, to detoxify just the twenty-two military vehicles hit by our own depleted uranium. There are, of course, thousands of such radioactive vehicles, buildings, and polluted sites in Iraq.

Not only Iraqis, but a quarter of a million Gulf War vets are sick with depleted uranium related illnesses and those military in Iraq today are also at risk. Some studies say that more than half of the returned Gulf War vets who have since had children have had babies born with serious birth defects—missing brains, organs, spines. Such deformed babies were also prevalent in the wake of Hiroshima and Nagasaki, and appear as well in communities settled near nuclear plants.

—

When I call my father, as I do nightly, I tell him that research I've done states that dust particles containing depleted uranium escaped from the National Lead Industries factory outside Albany, New York, and were swept by wind upstate in 1979. I expect him to react, as Albany is several hundred miles downstate from where he and my mother live, but he's nonplussed. For the first time, he tells me that as a graduate student he worked dipping rats into cobalt to see what the radiation did to their progeny. He liked doing this, he says, because while the rats were baking, he got to play handball. I am shocked by this news, but I laugh, because I can imagine my father back then, a Florida State football champion turned coach, dodging the draft by dabbling in biology at graduate school and electing to irradiate rats just so he could get a game in. I laugh, too, because my father knows, it seems, that it is useless to try to find the cause of his cancer. He has it, that's what's real, and for now he's simply trying to enjoy what he calls the 'lease on life' that his medication gives him.

—

Last summer I went home to help my mother plant and mulch 2,000 strawberry plants. We worked each day it didn't rain, the sun burning our backs, while my father dawdled around his herb garden. Sometimes, when I walked up the hill from the garden to the house to get a drink or to get out of the sun, I would come upon him sitting on a stone near the herb garden. I had never seen him rest during the day before. Ever since I can remember, he's worked like a madman, hauling stone here and there, hammering, sawing.

—

I wake up this morning aching for a lover. Such loneliness is extremely unflattering. Better to pose like artist Kenji Yanobe in a safe suit at the site of a radioactive city, looking out at the sunset, legs dangling from the ledge of an empty building. I love the photographs of Yanobe in his suit posing among the ruins of Chernobyl. In one shot, he sits alone in a nursery school classroom on a bed. The room is full of beds—metal springs exposed, child-sized mattresses strewn about the floor. A ripped out sink and a doll without limbs lie scattered in the photo's foreground. Only Yanobe's mouth is visible behind the glass portal of his mask. In the yellow suit and black rubber gloves and boots, he looks like a cross between a deep sea diver and a moonwalker, dressed for a dimension beyond the human. Yanobe's artistic sensibilities, his humor and otherwordly robotic aesthetic, are in line with the *superflat* style now popular in Japan, said to have come into fashion as a result of U.S. influence.

Postwar U.S. occupation of Japan is popularly understood as being linked to Japanese amnesia and destruction of memory. Americans, too, are said to have entered an age of numbing that began with Hiroshima. I wonder how numb I've become as I sit inside my room watching the world outside continue to whiten. Birds scamper around on top of my air conditioner. I lift my chiffon drape and look out at their ruffled black bodies and unicornish beaks as they peck away at the snow. They are hydrating. How, I wonder, can their bodies take in something so cold and they themselves not suffer from some sort of bird-hypothermia?

—

Where are you? Where you at? someone hollers outside.

I balance a hot tea on my thigh. Where am I?

I am in my room in Iowa City, trying to negotiate the isolation I've been experiencing more and more. I wonder if what I feel is anything like the isolation which affects those Japanese youth referred to as *hikikomori*, young upper-class individuals who withdraw into their bedrooms for years and spend most of their days online, obsessed with *anime* and *manga*. These recluses, who were born after the bomb, are not unlike many *hibakusha*—those badly scarred from the bomb—who also once refused to leave their homes, some staying inside their entire lives.

—

Snow fills the back of my truck. A bed of snow. Someone outside crunches his or her way across the ice. I pick up a book by concentration camp survivor Jean Améry on suicide. Améry (who later killed himself) writes about how the events that lead up to suicide cannot be expressed. But there is, he argues, sometimes logic behind the decision to die.

When he first got sick, my father wanted to be dropped into the middle of ice-cold Lake Champlain. Recently, however, he wrote to tell me he is losing some of his cynicism. He has always been cynical about the state of the world and this hasn't really changed, but he says he's learned something about the goodness of people from watching others who are sick live gracefully with cancer.

—

When I call him this evening, my father tells me my mother spent the day doing road maintenance. Shoveling? I ask, because I know my sixty-seven-year-old mother spends the days it snows shoveling the entire drive, even though my father has a backhoe with a plow.

No, more like whacking ice, my father laughs.

I got so lost in the work, my mom tells me when she gets on the phone, that I forgot to eat lunch, and I have a big old blister.

Her obsession with keeping the road clear began when my father fell ill. She's scared they won't be able to get out and make it to the hospital in an emergency.

There is something in her manic energy these days, though, that isn't always practical. I believe she dives into physical activity to numb herself, so as not to have to process or feel what is happening to my father. I think of her hands, punctured as they were by the hay from the mulch of the strawberries last summer. I recall, too, how thin she's become. And, as I remember her at the kitchen counter after working all day out in the field, fixing herself a coffee in her nightgown, her body barely there, a line from an American physicist's letter defending the atomic bomb's deployment comes to me: *I feel I should do the wrong thing if I tried to say how to tie the little toe of the ghost to the bottle from which we just helped it to escape.*

I think of Walter Benjamin who, while aware of technology's dangers, believed in the radical potential of mechanical reproduction. The excess materialism of our contemporary culture makes me question his belief. It seems utterly important now to reduce our replicating madness, or at least to hold such sickness at bay. Those of us who inhabit this virtual age might best work to unlock the secret of how to tie little toes to bottles—or in Benjamin's terms, although it goes against everything he argued, to attach auras (reverence) to lifeless, reproduced objects, as well as to virtual reproductions—as a way out of our numbness. My mother's voice grows faint. I tell her to take care.

AN ATLAS OF ILL-FITTING

Berger, John. *About Looking*. New York: Pantheon Books, 1980.

———*Pig Earth*. New York: Pantheon Books, 1980.

Sander, August. *People of the 20th Century: A Cultural Work of Photographs Divided into Seven Groups*. New York: Distributed by Harry Abrams, 2002.

———*August Sander: Photographs from the J. Paul Getty Museum*. Los Angeles: The J. Paul Getty Museum, 2000.

Wenders, Wim. *Notebook on Cities and Clothes*. [Video.] Troy, MI; Anchor Bay Entertainment, 2002.

AN ATLAS OF RESTRAINT

Genet, Jean. *Querelle*. New York: Grove Press, 1974.

Grandin, Temple. *Thinking in Pictures: My Life with Autism*. New York: Vintage Books, 2006.

————*Animals in Translation: Using the Mysteries of Autism to Decode Animal Behavior*. New York: Scribner, 2005.

Koestler, Arthur. *The Invisible Writing: An Autobiography*. Boston: Beacon Press, 1955.

Maharidge, Dale. *Denison, Iowa: Searching for the Soul of America Through the Secrets of a Midwest Town*. New York: Free Press, 2005.

Morris, Errol. *Mr. Death: The Rise and Fall of Fred A. Leuchter, Jr.* [Video.] Universal City, Calif.: Universal Studios Home Video, 2000.

Scully, Mathew. *Dominion: The Power of Man, the Suffering of Animals, and the Call to Mercy*. New York, NY: St. Martin's Press, 2002.

"Testimony of Guantánamo Detainee Jumah al-Dossari." *After Downing Street.org*. 18 July 2009. http://afterdowningstreet.org/detainee_Jumah_al-Dossari.

AN ATLAS OF THE ITINERANT NATURE OF PERSPECTIVE

Sebald, W. G. *The Rings of Saturn*. Trans. Michael Hulme. New York: New Directions Books, 1999.

What Was True: The Photographs and Notebooks of William Gedney. Eds. Margaret Sartor and Jeff Dyer. New York; London: Norton, 2000.

William Gedney Photographs and Writings. Rare book, manuscript, and special collections library. Duke University.

A BRIEF HISTORY OF ART IN THE CONGO

Art and Healing of the Bakongo, Commented by Themselves: Minkisi from the Laman Collection. Stockholm: Folkens Museum-Etnografiska; Bloomington, IN: Distributed in North America, 1991.

Brett, Guy. *Through Our Own Eyes: Popular Art and Modern History.* London: Gay Men's Press, 1987.

de Bock, Filip. "On Being Shege in Kinshasa: Children, the Occult and the Street." *Reinventing Order in the Congo: How People Respond to State Failure in Kinshasa.* Ed. Theodore Trefon. London: Zed Books, 2005.

Fabian, Johannes. *Remembering the Present: Painting and Popular History in Zaire.* Berkeley, Calif.: University of California Press, 1996.

MacGaffey, Wyatt. *Astonishment and Power.* Washington: published for the National Museum of African Art by the Smithsonian Institution, 1993.

Tshibumba Kanda Matulu. *The Dramatic History of the Congo as Painted by Tshibumba Kandu Matulu.* Amsterdam: KIT Publishers, 2005.

A BRIEF HISTORY OF BRONZE IN IRAQ

Bernhardsson, Magnus T. *Reclaiming a Plundered Past: Archaeology and Nation Building in Modern Iraq,* Austin: University of Texas Press, 2005.

Foster, Benjamin R. "Commemorative inscription ... Naram-Sin at Armanum." *Before the Muses: An Anthology of Akkadian Literature.* Bethesda, Maryland: CDL Press, 1993.

Foster, Benjamin R. and Karen Polinger Foster, and Patty Gestenblith, *Iraq Behind the Headlines: History, Archaeology, and War.* Singapore: World Scientific, 2005.

Meek, James. "The Sculptor: Kaled Izzat." *The Guardian.* 19 March 2004.

Muhly, James David. "The Tin Trade in the Aegean and Mesopotamia," in *Transactions,* vol. 43, New Haven, March 1973.

Offley, Ed. "Recycling Saddam." *Military.com.* 21 March 2004. http://
www.military.com/NewContent/0,13190,Defensewatch_031204_
Offley,00.html.

Shabout, Naba. "The 'Free' Art of Occupation: Images for a 'New'
Iraq." *Arab Studies Quarterly.* 22 June 2006.

THE AGE OF POSTCOLONIAL HANGING

Berger, John. "Twelve Theses on the Economy of the Dead." *Left Curve:
31.* Oakland, CA. http://www.leftcurve.org/LC31WebPages/LC31
Toc.html.

Breytenbach, Breyten. *The Memory of Birds in Times of Revolution.* New
York: Harcourt Brace, 1996.

"Bush Going For Broke with Troop Surge," *60 Minutes Exclusive,* Jan
14, 2007. http://www.cbsnews.com/stories/2007/01/13/60minutes
/main2358754_page4.shtml.

Jamail, Dahr. "Furor Over Saddam's Execution Continues Unabated,"
Dahr Jamail's Middle East Dispatches, Jan 16, 2007. http://www
.dahrjamailiraq.com/hard_news/archives/iraq/000527.php.

Lewis, John, Leon F. Litwack, and Hilton Als. *Without Sanctuary:
Lynching Photography in America.* Ed. James Allen. Santa Fe, N.M.:
Twin Palms, 2005.

Martin, William James. "Just How Evil Was Saddam Hussein?" *Media
Monitors Network.* 29 July 2003. http://www.mediamonitors.net/
williamjamesmartin2.html.

Minh-ha, Trinh T. *Surname Viet Given Name Nam.* [Video.] New York:
Women Make Movies, 2005.

Orwell, George. *Shooting an Elephant and Other Essays.* New York: Harcourt, Brace & World, 1950.

Taussig, Michael. *Walter Benjamin's Grave.* Chicago: University of
Chicago Press, 2006.

Benjamin, Walter. *The Arcades Project*. Cambridge, Mass.: Belknap Press, 1999.

——"The Work of Art in the Age of Mechanical Reproduction." *Illuminations: Essays and Reflections*. New York: Schocken Books, 1969.

——*Walter Benjamin's Archive: Bilder, Texte und Zeichen*. Frankfurt am Main: Suhrkamp, 2006.

THE AGE OF NUMBING

Abdelkrim-Delanne, Christine. "Not Such Conventional Weapons." *Le Monde diplomatique*. English edition. June 1999. http://mondediplo .com/1999/06/08duarms.

Al-Radi, Nuha. *Baghdad Diaries: A Woman's Chronicle of War and Exile*. New York: Knopf, 2003.

Anti-Flag. "Depleted Uranium Is a War Crime!!" http://www.youtube .com/watch?v=4RfNwdc6Lq4.

Améry, Jean. *On Suicide: A Discourse on Voluntary Death*. Bloomington: Indiana University Press, 1999.

Oe, Kenzaburo. *Hiroshima Notes*. New York: Marion Boyars, 1995.

van der Keur, Henk. "Radiant Iraq: Assassination by Conventional Nukes." *WISE News Communiqué*. 28 March 1998. http://www10 .antenna.nl/wise/387-8/radiant.html.

ACKNOWLEDGMENTS

The Age of Virtual Reproduction couldn't have been written without my having received an Iowa Arts Fellowship from the University of Iowa, nor without the expert midwifery services of my peers and professors there. In particular, I owe a heap of thanks to fellow writers Jennifer S. Cheng and April Freely who never stopped believing in my writing. Without their friendship and support throughout my two long years in Iowa, I would have edited these essays to death. Many thanks, as well, to Sam Hamill, editor of the Poets Against War website, for featuring "An Atlas of Restraint" on the website, and to the editors of *In Situ*, an Iowa City publication in which an early version of this same essay appeared. "A Brief History of Art in the Congo" was written while I was a writer-in-residence at the University Iowa Museum of Art, and I wish to thank the museum for providing me funding even after the 2008 flood temporarily shut the museum's doors. I also want to express gratitude to the Kopkind Colony for their retreat which brings people dedicated to working for justice together for radical discussion and relaxation. It was in preparation for this retreat that I pulled together my more radical essays into a bundle that I could share and first found the bones of this book. I then entrusted the work to Eula Biss, Catherine Taylor, and Stephen Cope, and it is my luck that they believed in it and guided me through its necessary revision. I'm so privileged to have been able to work with these astute, intellectually vigorous, passionate, unafraid editors. Endless thanks. Lastly, I'd like to thank those, as of yet unmentioned, who endured and spurred my idealism, and helped me hope and dream during the writing of this work: Al and Robin Ulmer, Nancy Hand, Arianne Burford, Rosalie Ehrlich, Di Wu, Leslie Van Wasserhove, Wanda Raiford, the Begley and Dixon families, Sahee Kil, Michael Bradfute, Hal Crowther, Tim Ostrom, Karekezi Sebanani, Josh Carney, and Sophia Beier. And for seeing me through the final edits, my profound gratitude to Dave Hollier.

ESSAY PRESS

Essay Press is dedicated to publishing innovative, explorative, and culturally relevant essays in book form. We welcome your support through the purchase of our books and through your donations directly to our press. We are a non-profit 501 (c)(3) organization. Please contact us at essaypress@gmail.com to be added to our mailing list and visit our website at www.essaypress.org.

EDITORS: Eula Biss, Stephen Cope, Catherine Taylor

ESSAY PRESS 208 Utica St. Ithaca, New York 14850

OTHER TITLES FROM ESSAY PRESS:
Jenny Boully *The Body*
Joshua Casteel *Letters from Abu Ghraib*
Albert Goldbarth *Griffin*
Carla Harryman *Adorno's Noise*
Jena Osman *The Network*
Kristin Prevallet *I, Afterlife: Essay in Mourning Time*